THE WILD WELSH COAST

100 YEARS AGO

EXPLORING

THE WILD WELSH COAST

100 YEARS AGO

SELECTED AND EDITED BY

STUART D. LUDLUM

THAMES AND HUDSON

OTHER TITLES IN THIS SERIES

EXPLORING CORNWALL
100 YEARS AGO

EXPLORING THE LAKE DISTRICT
100 YEARS AGO

EXPLORING SHAKESPEARE COUNTRY
100 YEARS AGO

Original article by Wirt Sikes first published in
Harper's New Monthly Magazine in 1883

This edition first published in Great Britain in 1985 by
Thames and Hudson Ltd, London

Printed and bound in Great Britain by
Butler & Tanner Ltd, Frome and London

FRONT COVER: CLIFFS NEAR ST DONAT'S CASTLE

CAMBRIAN CLIFFS AND CASTLES

WALES a century ago was a wilder land than now, in places primitive, remote, its people prone to superstition. And it was a land of contrasts: storm-lashed cliffs and sheltered havens, tiny hamlets and bustling commercial centres, abandoned ruins and fashionable resorts. Even more, it was the home of legends, saints and heroes, of Merlin, Sir Gawain and St David, of Llewelyn the Great and Owen Glendower.

It may be that the intrepid Victorian traveller was struck more acutely by the pleasures and surprises of the Welsh coastline—its landscape, fauna, people and buildings—than is the modern visitor; yet much remains unchanged. The age-old villages still occupy their prehistoric sites; the sea has never ceased to pound against the cliffs beneath St Donat's Castle, where wreckers used to ply their deadly trade; fortified church towers still dot the lovely Vale of Neath; the architectural glories of St David's continue, majestically, to survive; the fortress of Carreg-Cennen stands proud upon its precipice, its grandeur undiminished; and Ramsey Island remains the haunt of countless seabirds.

But changes there have been. Fishguard can hardly nowadays be called 'a dirty little fishing port', and the ridge of Cefn Bryn no longer forms a line of demarcation between the Welsh and English speakers of the Gower Peninsula, 'in dress, habits, character and appearance . . . completely unlike each other.'

Today's visitor, be it to Carmarthen, the ancient capital, more than ever over-shadowed by its upstart neighbour Llanelli, or to Amroth, where the sunken forest may still be seen at low tide, will find much enjoyment in comparing his own impressions with those of a less hurried and maybe more perceptive age.

NEARLY three-fourths of the entire circuit of Wales is sea-coast. A great part of this coast is rugged and dangerous, but there are frequently recurring harbors of refuge easily and safely entered. Steep and forbidding cliffs, with fronts of iron, black, jagged, frowning, receive the Atlantic's rudest buffetings grimly. The southern shore of Wales, from a point just below Cardiff to the extreme westernmost reach of land at St. David's Head, is washed by an ocean whose free sweep is unbroken straight across to the coast of Newfoundland. At various points the cruel cliffs are made still more cruel by huge disjected rocks scattered about at a distance from the mainland, as if the shore were showing its teeth in warning to the mariner. Where this frowning front is broken occur bights and bays of exquisite beauty, with long reaches of tawny sands which the waves lap lazily of a summer afternoon, or across which wild winds howl in storm. It is a striking line of coast, full of fascination in itself to the lover of the picturesque; but more : on every crowning summit stands a castle olden, looking seaward with its hoary façades

A WELSH STILE.

ing seaward with its hoary façades and battlemented towers—perhaps inhabited, perhaps crumbling still slowly away, as it has been crumbling for centuries. At every lovely harbor is an old-world village, or a great town with clanking hammers, the one rich, the other poor, but both dowered with those aspects of antiquity which are so dear to the eyes of the cultured American. There are villages along this wild Welsh coast of an ancientness to be equalled hardly anywhere else in Britain—villages which in some cases have undergone little change of aspect during the past five hundred years. Remote from railroads, primitive in all their ways, they are of the old world, olden. Time has hardly disturbed them since the days when London was a village too, with thatched roofs and winding lanes. In the caves and chasms hewed in the cliffs by the long rollers of the Atlantic thundering in a thousand storms have been found traces of primeval man—his bones, his implements, the bones of the

beasts he ate—in great abundance. The very land is older than the land of the English,
Scotch, and Irish. Ages before the solid parts of earth on which the rest of Britain
was built had risen above the wide waste of waters covering the world, this land,
now called Wales, stood alone in its glory, an island by itself, where strange monsters
dwelt, and misshapen birds and reptiles wandering left the tracks of their feet, which
are found to-day in the solid rock where they were imprinted countless ages ago.

The coast at Cardiff (where the sea arm which reaches up to the Severn is but a
dozen miles wide) is flat and rockless; but imme-
diately south of Cardiff rises a bold headland,
crowned with rural beauty. At low tide the feet
of this noble wall are bare, and you may walk
along the pebbly shore and look up its giddy
height; but in full tides and in stormy weather
the ocean's heaving field breaks high upon its
stony front, as if it would climb to the grassy
downs atop. In summer and in winter weather
I have trudged through the green lanes—always
green, even in midwinter—which lie within sight
and sound of the sea, behind Penarth Head, and
along the coast westward. You can not follow
the precise line of the shore, of course; there is no
road—even no foot-path, except at intervals—and
wide détours are forced upon you; but you are
never far from the sea. And onward through a
land of beauty you may walk, past many a ruined
castle and many a storied field, for many a long
summer day, following the windings and turnings
of the way, with the vast gray waters ever in sight.

The first really
formidable   cliffs
you encounter are
those which stand
near St. Donat's Cas-
tle, and are known

CLIFFS NEAR ST. DONAT'S CASTLE.

as the Nash Cliffs. These cruel rocks have been the scene of many shipwrecks in times both ancient and modern. Steamers and sailing vessels have been thrown against their rugged fronts and angles, and so mauled and broken that every soul on board has gone down to death, eager-eyed crowds on the shore beholding their fate, unable to save life, even when willing to attempt it. Numberless legends are related—stories fit to freeze one's blood—of the wicked old days when infamous wreckers lured ships to their doom with false lights on this shore. Like stories are told of many coasts in many countries. In the old days the superstitious dwellers by seashores deemed shipwrecked folk the abandoned and cast-out of Heaven, it is said; but one can hardly see just how their pious theory supported their knavish tricks, such as driving up and down the shore an ass bearing two lanterns in the night, whose motions seemed to the mariner like those of a distant vessel's lights, and drew him upon the rocks. When thus lured to destruction, and the sands strewn with his cargo, the unhappy sailor found no mercy from the wretches who made his goods their spoil. It was not alone the peasantry in the old days; the ancient lords of yon-

SOUTHERDOWN SANDS.

der castle of St. Donat's, which stands superbly on the adjoining height, made claim as a right to the spoils of wrecked ships which came ashore within the limits of their manor. Long after the laws of civilization had compelled the surrender of this claim, however, the lower classes continued to practice wreckage. All this is now happily a thing of the past. A light-house throws its broad glare far out to sea, and if people now cluster on the shore to watch the laboring of a vessel in the remorseless grasp of storm and wave, it is in sympathy and not in greed.

Now if I am expected to refer, even in the briefest terms, to all the castles and other antique remains which bristle upon the cliffs or crown the near-by hills upon our line of march, I must give great disappointment. To meet such an expectation is out of the question. I draw the line at such of these as I most closely inspected, and found most interesting or unique. St. Donat's Castle shares with a short dozen others the honor of mention here. With its haughty walls looking out over the expanse of waters stretching to the hills of Somerset on the one hand, and on the other straight away across the limitless ocean, embowered on its other sides in gorgeous depths of green, with its ancient church in the dell beneath it, directly under its overlooking battlements, and its crumbling watch-tower on the cliff, there are few more striking castle pictures in Europe. It is not a lonely ruin; it is inhabited by the surviving representative of the Norman paladin who built it, a gentleman of scholarly tastes and acquirements, proud of his castle, into possession of which he only came when in middle life, and which he has restored with long, loving, and learned care. "This key lets me through forty-eight doors," he said to me, jocularly, as he turned a huge key in its lock. The remark spoke eloquently of the extent of this mediæval military mansion, with its four and a half acres of roof. He pointed out to me the place on his lawn where Mr. Wesley stood and preached to five thousand people who were gathered on the broad terraces which drop down gracefully to the shore on the seaward front of the castle. Standing in a great bay-window, and looking out on this southern terrace, the ocean seems a stone-toss distant: it is really half a mile off, with lovely gardens stretching between, their ponds alive with gold-fish, their descending terraces bright with flowers, down and down to the walled paddock where a breastwork protects all from the ocean, and in old time protected it from the sea-rovers as well. As you walk in the lower part of the gardens, the ships that slide westward down the sea seem to be sailing in the sky.

I am conducted along a half-hidden by-path through the shrubbery under the castle wall, down the steep ravine, to the little church where sleep the ashes of a long line of Stradlings and of Carnes. The son of the present owner, Dr. Stradling-Carne, is presented to me as the twenty-eighth in descent from Sir William Stradling, and twenty-first in descent from Sir Devereux Carne. In a little chapel attached to the church are tablets of wood and of stone which tell the tales of the past in resonant inscriptions, and bear paintings of knights in armor and ladyes fayre.   Legends of romantic interest are among these records of the dead who slumber here; one of Sir Harry Stradling, Knight, who did go on a pilgrimage to Jerusalem, and who was captured on the sea in sight of his own castle of St. Donat's, by one Colyn Dolphyn, a pirate, who bled the knight of some two thousand marks redemption money.   "The wood has outlasted the stone," remarks my host; "I had to have that stone repaired," pointing to one much worn away.   But I observed that some of the wooden tablets were cracked down the middle.

The coast from St. Donat's to a point just before reaching Newton Nottage is very grand and picturesque, with towering cliffs, deep caves, and a magnificent swell of sea. One of those wind and tide phenomena which in various forms excite interest at several points on the Welsh coast is seen in a cave near Dunraven Castle, which stands on a cliff overlooking the sea, some one hundred feet above Southerdown Sands, a striking object in the distance, and surrounded by a lovely park.   The phenomenon is this: In the roof of a cavern some eighty feet deep are a number of holes which open on to the top of the cliff. When the tide is running strongly in, with a fresh wind from the southeast, a gust rushes up these holes with such force that articles held over them will be blown high into the air.

The line of cliff falls away after passing the Black Rocks, and the shore becomes tame and monotonous for some miles, the beach made up largely of drift sand. Here under sheltering wooded hills nestles Newton Nottage, one of the quaintest of forgotten villages, with its curious well, to which the more ignorant peasantry attach a mysterious significance, because its waters ebb

PULPIT IN NEWTON NOTTAGE CHURCH.

and flow with the sea, though high-water mark is half a mile distant, and the water in the well is as clear as crystal.   A cluster of women whom I found filling their water vessels at the well spoke of the matter laughingly; but nothing could surpass the seriousness with which the subject was treated by an old man I talked with in an inn at Porthcawl, the next village along the coast.   He could remember the time when the Beltane fires (he did not call them that) were lit near this well on Midsummer-eve, and the people jumped over the embers, for the good of the crops. The well was dedicated to St. John the Baptist, as also was the church near by it, and

NEWTON NOTTAGE CHURCH.

on St. John's eve (Midsummer-eve, June 23) the "fires of St. John" were from time immemorial lighted to drive away the dragons, at this time of year peculiarly offensive and terrible in the neighborhood of wells. In the church, which is ancient, is a remarkable stone pulpit, bearing a rude sculpture of the flagellation of Christ. It is a strange little box; a man of any inches can only get into it by stooping, groping about through the little stairway in the thickness of the wall. The small flight of steps to the right lead up to the rood-loft, where, however, nobody ever goes. I am writing, it must be remembered, of scenes unknown to the genus tourist.

In 1878 a discovery of much interest to American geologists was made at Newton Nottage. A wandering artist noticed upon a large slab of the Triassic conglomerate of the neighborhood, which covered a pool upon the village green, a series of six impressions made by the feet of some three-toed biped, which in all structural respects resemble the celebrated Brontozoum footprints described by Hitchcock and Deane as occurring at Abbottsville, Massachusetts, and Smith's Ferry, on the Connecticut, in a corresponding formation. The species has been described for the London Geological Society, and named *Brontozoum thomasi* (Sallas) after its finder, Mr. T. H. Thomas, the artist above mentioned. It seems to be almost identical with the American species, *B. validum* (Hitchcock). As being the only stone on which the im-pressions of the bird-footed reptiles of the Trias has as yet been discovered on the eastern side of the Atlantic, the Newton slab is deemed of great value, extending the known area of proto-ornithoid forms of life from longitude 72° to 4°. The slab was presented by its owner, Colonel Picton Turbervill, to the museum of the town of Cardiff.

Soon after leaving Newton Nottage, the lonely shore-running road taking us through Porthcawl and past Sker Point (a scene familiar to readers of Mr. Blackmore's novel, *The Maid of Sker*), we strike into the great highway which connects the chief towns of South Wales. It is a broad smooth road, with double hedges on either side, and its foundation is said to be in places actually the ancient Roman pavement of the Via Julia, which led from Caerleon (Isca Silurum)* through Neath (Nidum), Lloughor (Leucarium), and Carmarthen (Maridunum) to St. Davids (Menevia). Of these ancient burghs, Neath is presently at hand—a quaint old town, full of bustle on market-days, and the seat of a considerable commerce. The Vale of Neath, which stretches back inland, is renowned for its natural beauties, its water-falls, ravines, glens, brooks, cliffs, caverns, and bosky depths. But to reach this land of beauty the rambler must turn his back on the sea, and climb yonder hills,

* For an account of Caerleon, see article, "On the Usk," in *Harper's Magazine* for May, 1877.

whose bosoms are full of the mineral wealth on which Neath town doth thrive. On a flat stretch of land in our direct way stand the ruins of an ancient abbey, once "the fairest in all Wales," the old chroniclers tell, but now blackened and begrimed, amid surroundings of the most utilitarian character — canals, tall chimneys, coal-pits, and miscellaneous mineral litter. I lingered an afternoon in the romantic recesses of this lovely ruin—for it is lovely within, however much its outward walls may have lost of their first beauty—a bower of charm to the æsthetic sense in the midst of a dirty money-grubbing eye-soreness, which is quite shut out when once you are within its ivy-hung inclosure. No soul greeted my sight while there; the porter's wife stood in her door as I passed through the guest-house entrance, and suggested that she would be pleased to take "wotever you like to give," and then I was quite alone for the rest of the day. It is not a frequented spot, I should say, this abbey of Neath. I wandered where I would, unquestioned by the suggestive solitude. Now and then I found a locked door, but I climbed through ivied windows, or pushed my way between rusty iron bars, and stood in the silence of huge fire-places with mantels far above my head, and looked up at the blue summer sky through vast broken chimneys. Dim religious lights soften the gloom of these interiors. Strange shadows play upon their smooth bare walls, reflected from the breast of the stream which glides noiselessly under the paneless windows.

Of course there is also a castle at Neath, once a grand place, with a grand history; but its ruins are less interesting than the old church tower. What a tower is this! Of course it was built with less regard to beauty than to its probable use as a military defense, a place of refuge for the people in case of an assault from some marauding band of sea-rovers. It is presumed that the present door and windows have been cut in the old walls lately; usually these military church towers can only be entered through the church. Along the entire coast of Wales certain striking characteristics are observed in the churches. Here is a group of Welsh churches; look at their towers, each more ponderous than the next. It needs no argument to convince us they were meant for strongholds as well as campaniles. They could almost defy the waves of ocean, like the cliffs; have done so, indeed, in certain instances when the seas have risen in storm and fury, and plunged roaring inland to the church doors. The aspect of these places of worship is well in keeping with the shore scenery to which they give character. The rough weather they are often doomed to encounter in their generally exposed situations, is provided against by an entire absence of external ornamentation, and a rugged solid simplicity of construction. Many of them have been restored in the present century—some rather too much restored; but others err in this regard by omission rather than commission. The feelings of the antiquary are offended by the introduction of incongruous pointed or staring square-headed windows and such like base insertions; but even this is more endurable than the neglect which has been allowed to fall on many of these old sea-coast temples.

The town of Swansea disputes alone with Cardiff the title of Metropolis of Wales. Its right to be called the "metallurgical capital" none will question. Its situation is very fine, between lofty hills, on a bay so lovely that it has often been compared to that of Naples. The streets are full of life and bustle, and greatly suggest certain busy quarters of London in their aspect. Cabs dart and drays trundle heavily to and fro; the quays resound with the voice of labor; a forest of masts bristles against the sky. Nowhere in England may be found more superb private residences as evidences of wealth in the town; example Singleton Abbey, a seat of the Vivian family, influential in numberless ways in Swansea, and well known in America, where they have important connections. In the midst of the town, quite in its busiest part, stand the ruins of Swansea Castle, so pushed and elbowed by modern thrift that they seem quite out of place and down-hearted. They are so hidden, too, that no one sees them unless taking special pains to do so. The grim old keep stands there, still adorned with its elegant open parapet of arches, but black, mossy, and weed-grown atop, looking down mournfully on the crowding shops and busy offices, the brisk new buildings on the one hand, the old tumble-down houses on the other (things of to-day to it), with their jutting lamps and stony gutters beneath, in Castle Lane.

The copper-smoke cloud which hangs

over a part of Swansea, and which blasts the vegetation over which it hangs, while not an addition to the attractions which draw the eye, is the banner of its commercial prosperity. The town is indeed the copper metropolis of the queendom. Copper smelting was introduced here as early as 1090, when the ores were brought over in boats from Cornwall and Devon, but now ores come from every part of the world, including the United States. The most extensive tin-plate factories on earth are also at Swansea; not to speak of factories for the handling of gold, silver, zinc, lead, nickel, cobalt, alkali, arsenic, and other minerals. Iron, too, is an active agent in Swansea's bustle.

Climbing to the top of one of the high hills which overhang the town, close on its busy streets—indeed, the streets climb a good way up the hill itself—you get a good bird's-eye view of Swansea. Off to your left is the great smoke cloud, into which hurrying trains are constantly disappearing. Below the hill on which you stand, spread upon a broad plateau, or what seems such from this height, though many of those streets are steep to climb, the town lies, a wide sea of roofs, bordered with a fringe of masts, and disappearing yonder to the right around the hills Mumbles-ward. Beyond lies the ocean, smooth in the summer sun, dotted with sails, a field of gleaming sunshine and rippling shadow.

Do you know what the Mumbles are? Out of the sea rise two rocks side by side, very nearly alike in shape, to which the term Mammal was applied by the Romans in the first century. From this came in the course of time Mammals and Mumbles. Thus, at least, say the scholars, and point to other like terms in lands where the Roman sway has left its traces. At low tide the nearer-shore rock is quite laid bare, and one may even walk out to the second rock, on which stands Mumbles Head Light-house. But the waves dash high upon these rocks when the tide is in. They shelter the little harbor, and make it a refuge for vessels of light tonnage in stress of weather. The light-house throws a light twenty miles out to sea. Under the rock on which it stands is a cave, one of a series which have made this peninsula famous. There is no point on the coast where there are so many caves so near together, and some of them still yield bones and other traces of prehistoric man.

Locally, they are called holes—as Bacon Hole, Minchin Hole, etc.

One does not walk from Swansea to the Mumbles. There is a *quantum suff.* of that best of medicines, walking, before the most indefatigable pedestrian after reaching the Mumbles, and it is to be taken *nolens volens*, moreover. Conveyances of any sort are rarely to be found in the rural parts of the Land of Gower, and it is into these parts of that famous land we strike on leaving the Mumbles to follow the coast. We do not walk to the Mumbles, but take the tramway, which runs along the level beach. Concerning this tramway there are curious facts. It lay buried for a generation under the sea-sands which had drifted over it, the rails having been put down before George Francis Train was born—too early, indeed, for the British mind, which did not favor the notion. at all. The time came, however, when the buried rails were inherited by a man who proceeded to sweep the sand off them, and put on a car or two of a home-made sort, original in architecture. This time the enterprise flourished, and in August, 1877, upon the first tramway rails ever laid down in Wales, horses were superseded by the first tramway engine introduced into the principality.

The Land of Gower occupies a broad headland running out into the sea between the Bay of Swansea and Carmarthen Bay. It is founded on a mass of old red sandstone conglomerate, flanked north and south by strata of carboniferous limestone. Its coast is broken up into a remarkable series of picturesque coves, caves, chasms, bluffs, gulfs, strange rock formations; the ruins of several mediæval castles look out to sea from its cliffs and hills; remains of Roman encampments are on its mountains; while as for traces of prehistoric man, it is famous for what it has yielded, and still yields. Travellers seldom penetrate into this old-world Land of Gower. There are no railroads, and few carriage-roads; none but the foot-passengers can move quite freely about. There are, perhaps, a few inns which can entertain a man with beer and bread and cheese, but it is unsafe to count on much more; so that no stranger who objects to "roughing it" in a mild sort of way will venture far into Gower, unless he goes on a visit to one of the wealthy lords of the soil, who have here, as everywhere in Britain, their lovely country-seats. The people who inhabit

THE MUMBLES.

this peninsula present the singular phenomenon of an alien people completely occupying a region in the heart of Wales. Gower was invaded, at a comparatively late period of history, by a race of another blood, and effected a complete substitution of themselves, with their own tongue and their own ways, for the original inhabitants. Until lately there was a clearly defined line to be drawn at a certain point across the peninsula, on one side of which was the Welsh language, on the other the dialect of English spoken by these Flemish descendants. There was no bilingual ground: here Welsh was spoken by all; just beyond, by none. A similar state of things prevails in Pembrokeshire, on the other side of Carmarthen Bay. What became of the Welsh inhabitants when these Flemish came has been a curious question. The line of demarkation (more vague now, but still existent) is the mountain ridge called Cefn Bryn. The races dwelling in the separated districts have been close neighbors for some eight centuries, but are still less amalgamated than the polyglot population of the United States; in dress, habits, character, and personal appearance they are still completely unlike each other. But, as a whole, they are a peculiarly thrifty and self-respecting people, these so-divided Gowerlanders. The percentage of out-door paupers in Gower is the lowest in Wales. As for

15

in-door paupers, they are so insignificant a percentage of the population that no account is taken of them in the returns.

As you are preparing to climb the acclivity leading over the hills to Langland Bay, your attention is arrested by the fact that a considerable commerce in donkey hire prevails at the Mumbles, for as far as the Mumbles, it is needless to say, not only the genus tourist but the genus excursionist does penetrate, since it is merely a tram-ride from Swansea. Concluding to try this mode of progression, you select the least diminutive of the donkeys and the most wide awake of the boys in charge thereof, and, bestriding the former, begin the ascent under the auspices of the latter. The boy scampers by your side, and while encouraging the donkey with thwacks, entertains the rider with converse, thus enabling you to study the dialect of the region. It closely resembles that which is spoken in Somersetshire, and also that which you later hear in Pembrokeshire.

"Beant 'un a purty donkey, zur? [Whack.] 'Er name be Jennie."

"Not so pretty as her name," you reply. "And what is your own name?"

"John Spry, zur."

"Are you Welsh?"

"Noa, zur."

"Do you speak any Welsh?"

"Noa, zur; a wouldn't larn it."

"Ah, there you are wrong, John Spry. It is better to have two languages than one."

"Has you got two lang'ages, zur?"

"I? A dozen."

"Loor, zur!"

Between two particularly energetic whacks John Spry remarks that he himself owns Jennie.

"Indeed! Valuable property, isn't she?"

"A cost two pun ten, zur," is the proud reply.

"You make a deal of money, I dare say."

"A good bit, zur. It do cost a lot to keep 'un, though."

"How much does it cost?"

"Oh, a lot."

"But what amount per week?"

"Oh, a good bit. Oh, much."

No clearer figures than these can you get from John Spry.

Jennie has a propensity for stopping for repose, and you find that if you do not resist this purpose in its earlier stages, it is followed by the retirement of the brute upon its haunches—an attitude quite incompatible with a good seat on the rider's part. Therefore you adopt the expedient of assisting Jennie along with your umbrella, after the fashion of a walking-stick, and as your toes are almost on the ground (the beast is so small) you present the appearance, to a casual observer, of a person walking up-hill with a donkey between his legs. But you presently find yourself at the top of the hill overlooking Langland Bay, and permit the donkey to sit down permanently as you walk away to the edge of the bluff.

Langland is one of those pretty little bays of which I have spoken, so frequently occurring along the whole line of coast—a lovely sheltered spot, with farm-houses, elegant country-seats, and "bathing-boxes" (as the sea-side cottages are called) perched about on the green hill-sides or the level coast. The place is a popular bathing resort for Swansea folk who do not care to go further; but there are painful stories of life lost here, through bathers' carelessness and

"the remorseless outdraught of the sea."

Here commences our long tramp through the Land of Gower, pursuing the sea-coast. By striking directly across the peninsula one could reach the nearest railway station on the opposite side in a two hours' walk. We shall be as many days following the coast around to the same point, but it is the coast which attracts in Gowerland. The rugged pile of stones upon the cliff which arrests attention ere we have walked far has an enchanted reputation. It is what remains of a famous castle called Pennardd, whose history is lost in oblivion. The fancy of the ignorant peasant has freer play concerning a castle of which nothing definite is known. Tradition relates that Pennardd was built in a single night by the hand of an enchanter. It is believed to be still haunted by troops of fairies, who hold mad revels in its grass-grown precincts on summer nights. It was destroyed, the legends say, as it was built, in a single night, by a tornado of Irish sand blown across the sea by malignant Hibernian genii, and all that remains to tell the tale of its former grandeur are two round towers and some fragments of embattled wall. I was fortunate enough to secure a very close photograph of this fairy castle; the distinctness with which the coarse strong stones of the structure are outlined by the camera is peculiarly interesting in view of their magical origin.

Looking out to sea from its perch on the side of the mountain ridge called Cefn Bryn stands Arthur's Stone, renowned from time immemorial as one of the Seven Wonders of Wales. The erection of this stone where it now stands is mentioned in the *Triads* as one of the Three Arduous Undertakings that were accomplished in the isle of Britain, the building of Stonehenge was another, and the third was the formation of an unknown pile in some unknown place. Romantic traditions in great number surround this stone; one of these ascribes its erection to the prodigious strength of King Arthur. A common fancy would let this suffice: Arthur by his mighty arm heaved the stone into position. In view of the fact that it is fourteen feet long and seven feet thick, and must weigh many tons, the task were enough for one man, even an Arthur. But a Welsh fancy could never content itself with so simple a thing as this, so it was from a mountain-top miles away that Arthur tossed this pebble here one day as he was strolling by. Another superstitious belief still widely credited is that the stone was set up as an altar for human sacrifice by the Druids, who had beneath it a sacred well, and around it a forest of mystic oaks. There is no well under the stone, nor can one see how there could ever have been one. There is no trace of a forest having been here at any time. That the interesting object was ever placed here by human agency is of course a baseless fancy. The stone is a mass of millstone grit, stranded upon the old red of the mountain ridge thousands upon thousands of years ago, a mute witness of the geological epoch when these mountains were sunk beneath the level of the sea. In the walk from Arthur's Stone to Oxwich Church, near by, we pass the Oxwich salt-marshes.

The most interesting point on the Gower coast is a rocky promontory called Worm's Head. They tell us that sailors who see it from the westward perceive in

ARTHUR'S STONE, AND THE SALT-MARSHES OF OXWICH.

FISHING FROM CORACLES.

it a resemblance to a great worm crawling with head uplifted—a thing they naturally would do if they already knew its name, which is probably a corruption. From other points of view the head is thought to resemble other objects, as a great mile-stone, a lion couchant, a camel, etc. The promontory runs more than a mile out to sea, and at half-flood becomes an island, the isthmus connecting it with the mainland being then submerged by the tide. Its sea-front is some three hundred feet perpendicular. A series of strange phenomena characterize it. There are times, in quite calm and bright weather, the sea lying almost without a ripple, when the waves of the ocean come climbing mysteriously up the sides of this precipice in a dense volume, surmounting it, and breaking over its summit in a vast cascade. The fishermen say this strange performance is the result of a meeting of opposing under-currents, and is the sure precursor of a storm. The Head is hollow; inside is a great cavern, very dangerous to enter, but which has been entered, nevertheless, by one rowing a boat within on a quiet summer day, and rowing out again with some haste. The winds and waves habitually hold such dissolute revels inside the cavern of this haughty Head that a boat which should be caught in there by so much as a wandering zephyr from the sea would have a very hard time of it. The winds become transformed to furies in this roaring abode of chaos. Long before a storm has really arisen, the most terrific turmoil is raging inside the Head, and through an opening in the rock above—a little crevice no wider than a man's two fingers, and no longer than his arm—there rushes a torrent of tempestuous wind, with a noise like the blowing of a furnace. This noisy monitor utters the warning of an approaching storm. Science has dubbed it the Rhossilly Barometer (Rhossilly is the weather-beaten little village hard by); the people call it simply the Blow-Hole; and if ever snake's head should attain such dimensions as this Head of Worm, its hiss would perhaps be as loud as the noise of this Head's blow-hole. The cause of the noise is of course simple, and needs no explanation; it has abundant parallels at many points on the Welsh coast. The Head is haunted by many a wild legend—of a great door in the depths of the cave, studded with mighty nails, and which is heard to bang and slam noisily in storms; of terrible shipwrecks, centuries ago, of proud Spanish galleons, which went down laden heavily with treasure, sowing the sands with golden coins, which men still dig up from time to time; of the ghost of the lord of the manor, who was stabbed on the shore, with his hands full of Spanish gold, and who haunts the Head o' nights in a phantom chariot drawn by four black horses.

The shores of Carmarthen Bay are low, marshy, and sandy, except on the western side, where they rise again in commanding cliffs. At Llanelly we enter Carmarthenshire, the largest county in Wales, and the least explored in modern times. The English tourist knows comparatively little about this county; the American tourist, nothing. It is the centre of many interesting and unique peculiarities of Welsh life, and has something like a dozen ruined castles, closely associated with the most fascinating stories of Welsh history. Its legends and traditions go ages further back than its authentic history does. The cave in which Merlin was buried alive by the siren with whom he was in love, and the rocky chair upon the hill-side from which he delivered his prophecies, are still pointed out to strangers. The cave is certainly the same cave which has been hallowed (or diabolized) by the memory of Merlin for many centuries. Beyond this fact it is not needful to go. The people of Carmarthenshire retain the primitive aspect and manners of old Wales in an unusual degree. The Welsh language is universally spoken. To many of the smaller towns the English language has hardly penetrated. The women wear the old Welsh peasant costume to an extent common nowhere else in Wales that I have seen. Old-fashioned social customs still prevail. The fishermen still use the coracle—a kind of boat obsolete in less primitive regions. The old Welsh songs are sung by the bards, the old Welsh tunes played by the harpers, the old Welsh superstitions linger in the vales and mountains, the old Welsh love of Wales and all things Welsh burns with an ardor which seems undying and indestructible. By its history, by its manners and customs, by the spirit of the people, Carmarthenshire is Welsh of the Welsh. One unacquainted with the people who inhabit different parts of Wales might suppose, on looking at the map of Great Britain, that there is at least one county which would exhibit even stronger Welsh peculiarities than Carmarthen. It is clear enough that Carmarthenshire is the part of Wales most remote from England, and therefore least likely to feel the English influences—with one exception, to wit, Pembrokeshire. But the fact is that Pembrokeshire is the least Welsh of any county in Wales; its people are like the people of Gowerland. So far as regards its strongly national characteristics, Pembrokeshire might almost as well be cut off from the mainland, and towed across the Channel, and tacked on to Devonshire, thus leaving Carmarthenshire's western border an unbroken seacoast.

Carmarthen town was in old time a grand place—the capital of all Wales— the seat of the Welsh Parliament, Chancery, Exchequer, and Mint. Here Welsh sovereigns long held their court; the royal residence was in a castle whose only remains now are seen in an irregular broken wall or two, without apparent form or purpose. But Carmarthen's ancient glories have departed. On the eastern edge of the county has sprung up a young upstart of a rival, Llanelly—not above a paltry three or four hundred years old— which has taken a great deal of the wind out of the sails of its older neighbor. Llanelly is not a very great town as yet: but then consider its youth! It is so far superior to Carmarthen, however, that the United States recognizes it as a consular point, while it utterly ignores the ancient capital. Swansea, Llanelly, and Milford Haven are the only points on the Welsh coast where the United States has deemed it essential to establish agencies, dependencies of the Cardiff consulate. There is little beyond this fact to call us to Llanelly: it has no history; it is too new. The history of Wales was already finished when that of the United States began. After dark the town of Llanelly is picturesque by reason of its great copper and iron works, which resound with the thunder of steam-hammers and glow red with fire. I strolled about for an hour in the evening, fascinated by the sight of these buildings aflame in the night, their iron skeletons outlined in the gloom by the roaring fires within, their chimneys belching like volcanoes. The laborers' wives stood bare-headed in the dusky streets,

chatting in groups.   Before a cheery coal fire,
in an inn across the way from the foundries, I
found a cluster of forgemen sitting and smok-
ing, each with his blue earthen mug of beer
before him, the room lighted only by the bright
blaze of the fire on the hearth, the thud of the
engines over the way shaking the solid earth
on which the stone inn stood.   Yet in Llanelly there
are handsome residences, the abodes of a cultivated
and refined people, among whom literature and
the arts flourish.   There is an Atheneum, and
there is a musical society which
cultivates Handel and Beetho-
ven; and in testimony
of the fasci-
nations   of
its fair sex
there is the

OXWICH CHURCH.

verse of Savage, who celebrated the charms of a bux-
om widow Jones of Llanelly
a hundred years ago.   Ten miles from
Llanelly stands a town to walk whose
streets is to be set dreaming of thousand-
year-old things.   A quaint collection of
weather-beaten stone houses are those
which line the narrow and irregular streets
of Kidwelly.   It is divided in two by the
river Gwendraeth (white strath), and one part is called the new town, the other the old
town.   The new town, quotha!—it was old and moss-grown when Columbus discovered America.   In it stand a church hoary with age, some ruins of a priory, and
several houses of great antiquity, all of which become insignificant in the presence
of the lion of the old town.   We reach the old town by crossing an ancient and narrow bridge, and there, upon a rocky eminence on the river-bank, stands the lion
referred to—Kidwelly Castle.

Among the ruins of Wales, Kidwelly stands pre-eminent as a specimen of har-
monious castle architecture.   There is a symmetry in its outlines which lifts it

above the level of Welsh castles generally, from an artistic point of view. The old castle - builders of Wales were seldom guided by the purpose of producing works which should win from nineteenth - century critics the honor of being dubbed an "architectural composition." They aimed at strength, and they achieved majesty— a fortress which should excite the admiration, wonder, and awe of the vulgar, and defy the assaults of armed hordes, was their ideal castle, and they troubled themselves little about symmetry of whole. In the case of Kidwelly, however, they seem to have builded better than they knew— or intended. Instead of being an unintelligible mass, the arrangement of its towers and walls is orderly. On every side the face of strength looks down upon you: there is a frowning tower in every point of view; yet the whole effect is grace.

There are few ruined castles in Wales which have sustained so little injury as Kidwelly. None of its walls or towers seem to have been blown up, although its lead, iron, and timber have been carried off, and their place supplied with a luxuriant growth of ivy. One mural tower has tumbled into the fosse, but it was overturned by the hand of time alone: there was something wrong with its foundations. Yet few castles have had a stormier history.

Across the bay stands another castle, which affords a striking contrast to Kidwelly in several respects. The bay is narrow here, and the waters of the river Towy mingle with those of the sea under the gloomy walls of Llanstephan castle. We do not need to cross the bay in order to have the best of this mysterious ruin; the picture it presents on its precipitous height, at whose feet the sea breaks, is its best point. It has stood in sombre loneliness, just as it stands now, mysterious and voiceless, ever since the days when Robin Hood was making merry in Sherwood Forest. A lovely country stretches hence to the old town of Carmarthen. However primitive may be the ways of the people in the heart of Wales, the land everywhere gives evidence of tasteful culture. The landscapes in all directions appeal eloquently to whatever we may possess of the æsthetic spirit. Nowhere in Wales can you find a spot where exist those horrible outrages on the natural beauties of scenery which are so common in America. It is a mat-

ter for constant thankfulness, as we wander about these hills and vales, that never once is the sight offended by seeing a patent-medicine legend on a rock, a blacking advertisement on a fence, even a handbill on a tree. There are proper places appointed for bill-posting, and bills are posted nowhere else. As for the stentorian letters which glare and bellow and scream at us in America from every cliff face as we whirl through the land by rail, there is nothing of the sort in the country which belongs to the " nation of shop-keepers." (This libel is not often heard nowadays.) I shudder to think, as I roam among these grand old castles, along these rock-bound shores, that if they were in America they would be plastered all over with quack advertisements by my enterprising countrymen. The scene we traverse in drawing near Carmarthen has no fences to tempt patent-medicine paint-pots ; green hedges run everywhere, from mountaintop to sea-coast. The smooth river Towy winds placidly through a land of peace and grace. There is near the town a bend of the stream so round and symmetrical that Giotto might have drawn it, or Hogarth created it with a sweep of the pencil which struck the famous line of beauty.

No town in Wales made at first sight so strange and strong an impression on my mind as Carmarthen. Caerleon came near to it in this regard. Caerleon, however, is a village on a plain, while Carmarthen is a large town, with steep narrow streets climbing about in never-ending vicissitude, and it seems like some quainter and older corner of old London—London as it was in Hogarth's day, I mean. Carmarthen has stood still for centuries. The busy hand of improvement is ever at work on London, whose most ancient relic of ancient time, the Tower, looks as if it were sponged all over with water and wiped off with a towel every day of its life. I first came upon the Tower direct from my studies among Welsh castles; I had never seen it before, and by contrast with the picturesque ruins with which I had been hobnobbing in Wales, the Tower of London seemed as void of antique poetic aspect as an American penitentiary. Not a tuft of ivy upon it; not a broken wall about it ; everything patched and mended to perfection ; nowhere a glimpse of delightful old dirt, picturesque rubbish, mossy windows; everywhere order, neatness, and wholeness. What the careful hand of man, the march of progress, has wrought on this old historic building, it has wrought with even greater obduracy elsewhere throughout London. But in the ancient Welsh capital,

as sung the "Polyolbion," two hundred years ago—modern enterprise has little disturbed the atmosphere of ancientness. So at least I found it. If in a dream I had been taken back into the past, and set down in a city of Queen Anne's reign, it could hardly have been more strange and fascinating to me than certain quarters of Carmarthen proved. And this was not because of any special picturesqueness in its historical relics. Indeed, there is hardly a town in Wales where these relics are so few. The castle, rich with historic interest, is almost obliterated; over the walls of the county jail you may catch sight of some poor piles of moss-grown stone, and that is all. There are also in the town some traces of an old priory, and in the church some ancient tombs. Beyond these, nothing. Yet the very air is heavy with antiquity, and at every street corner I paused to look about me with an interest too profound for words. The town seems peopled with the ghosts of greatness, the shades of mighty men who have walked its streets, from Roderic the Great, first King of all Wales, to Llewellyn the Great, last of her native princes; from Merlin the Enchanter to St. David, holiest of Welshmen; not to name such modern-like men as Owen Glendower, who captured the town in 1403, and the immortal Beau Nash, pink of Welshmen, who was a school-boy here in the seventeenth century. In St. Peter's Church sleep the remains of Sir Rhys ap Thomas, who, Welsh historians claim (and with a good showing, too), slew Richard III. on Bosworth Field, and of Sir Richard Steele, who died in Carmarthen in 1729. This church is as rugged and unlovely as the weather-beaten face of one of Cromwell's sternest Puritans. It is surrounded by a grave-yard, through which runs a pathway that seems to be a short-cut from one busy quarter of the town to another, and generally has a lawyer's clerk or two rushing through it, with pen behind ear, as careless of his surroundings as if he were in Nassau Street, New York. There were some quaint old ladies from the rural dis-tricts loitering among the graves; it happened to be a cattle-show day, and the "hill-folk" were about everywhere, clad in their queer petticoats and cloaks, and wearing the tall beaver hats which are the special badge of the Welsh peasant women. There were more women in the streets with these hats than without them; and I am inclined to think the antique costumes of the women, and the knee-breeched men I everywhere met, had something to do with producing on my mind that strong impression of by-gone times of which I have spoken. A greater variety of knee-breeches and gaiters, Pickwickian and others, I do not remember to have seen anywhere.

Near Carmarthen is the extraordinary ruin of Carreg-Cennin. This castle stands on the summit of an insulated rock, whose entire area—about an acre—it completely covers with its walls. The perpendicular cliff upon whose top the ruins tower is on three sides a sheer precipice of three hundred feet, utterly inaccessible; and the castle walls being themselves uncommonly tall, the outlook from their battlements into the yawning gulfs all about is enough to make the most veteran climber turn giddy.

In following the sea-shore, we reach at Laugharne Castle the boundary line dividing Wales from the part of Pembroke-shire which for centuries has been dubbed "Little England beyond Wales." The state of things described as existing in Gowerland is repeated here, but on a larger scale. For seven centuries this castle has marked the point beyond which the Welshman and the Fleming have refused to go, either in his way—never intermarrying, understanding not each other's language, and as completely divided in thought and feeling as if a high wall ran between them. The castle stands directly on the shore, where the river Taff falls into the sea. On the landward side it is very lovely, its hoary walls being richly hung with ivy, and its towers strongly outlined against the background of water and sky.

At Amroth is an example of the submerged forests which are found at various points along the coast. At low spring-tides may be seen the roots and stumps of ancient forest trees sticking up out of the sand. On being handled, the wood generally crumbles to pieces, but in some instances it is firm and sound. Scraping

CARREG-CENNIN—MORNING MIST.

down into the sand, you come upon
the ancient soil in which these forest trees stood, and in this dark
earth are found nuts, leaves, and
twigs which centuries ago grew on
these trees and fell from them, as well
as bits of the insects which lived on
them.   Welsh tradition tells how vast
tracts of land on the coast of Wales
were in old times overflowed by the
sea, forests, farms, and villages swal-
lowed up, through the keeper of the
sluices one day getting on a drunken
spree, and leaving the sea-gates open.
But geologists know that the sea-level
never alters, and those submerged lands
have simply sunk.   The restless sea,
with its ever-shifting tides, its leaping
and plunging hills and valleys in storm,
is in fact changeless from age to age;

TENBY, FROM THE CLIFF.

but the firm land on which we dwell has been upheaved and submerged again and again, its rude rocks tilted, broken, and crumpled, its level strata turned up on end like rows of books on a shelf, or squeezed into wild contortions. The changeless sea laughs at the "eternal hills" of Wales, knowing they are as things of yesterday, even though they are ages older than the snow-clad Alps.

On the western shore of Carmarthen Bay we come upon the most celebrated of Welsh watering-places, Tenby, surmounting a rocky peninsula of mountain limestone about eleven hundred yards long, and rising from Castle Hill gradually up to a point some one hundred feet above the sea-level. This hill is the public pleasure-ground of the town, and is laid out as a park, with a fine statue of Prince Albert in the middle, looking ever toward the town, his back to the sea. The place holds a fashionable crowd in summer, and is the Long Branch of Wales—if I may compare a town which is commonplace of aspect with one whose every view is picturesque in the extreme. Nowhere perhaps does the Welsh coast gambol with wilder eccentricity than at and about Tenby. The stratification of rocks and cliffs exhibits forcibly the upheavals of the earth above referred to, being now oblique, now perpendicular, again crumpled into wave lines. Where the perpendicular stratification occurs, the cliffs are broken at their base into a wondrous variety of strange fantastic forms. The action of the sea on these upright strata is constantly producing changes in the configuration of the coast. Not only are the cliffs worn into caves and funnels, but huge piles are segregated from the mainland, and bored into arches, needles, and other picturesque forms. Wild tragedies endow all these natural wonders with intensest human interest; strange legends of sea-genii also haunt them. When the tide is high, and you visit them by boat,

THE KEEP AND SALLY-PORT, PEMBROKE.

if the water is very quiet—as it sometimes is for many summer days together in sheltered bays—its transparency permits you to look down into the depths to the feet of precipices where the purple-ringed medusæ are playing.

Of ruined castles there are many hereabouts, but that which before all others on this coast commands attention is the magnificent pile at Pembroke. The walk thence from Tenby is a delightful one, the country luxuriant in the extreme, though so near

ST. GOWAN'S CHAPEL.

the sea. Sometimes you may saunter on for miles between the tall hedge-rows towering on each side far overhead, throwing the road into deep and grateful shade. A part of this road I traversed seated by the side of an intelligent man of the peasant class from Pembrokeshire. "*Not* Welsh, no, zur," he remarked, emphatically, in answer to my query on that point. The utilitarian mind of my driver was made strikingly apparent when I commented on the beauty of the hedge-rows, intimating that they were a feature to American eyes inexpressibly dear in a landscape, and surely made half the charm of the incomparable rural scenery of Britain. "Ye', zur," he said, looking at the hedge-rows as if they had never before presented themselves to his mind in this new light; "they's a great waste o' land, zur, be hedges."

Into Pembroke town trundling, we drew up before the Golden Lion Inn. And what a quaint old town is Pembroke! It almost equals Carmarthen in the charm of the antique, but it is much smaller. Its modern importance is derived from Pembroke Dock, a newer town which has sprung up in connection with the government works, where the largest British men-of-war are built. The towering walls of the castle back every vista in the old town. We enter the broad green court-yard; it is a well-kempt place; the grass is tidy and close-cropped; the surrounding walls are clean, though richly ivied. Here are a fine old banqueting-hall, a curious chapel, a cavern opening on the bluff, and so on. All other features quite give way before the supreme interest of the mighty round tower which lifts its majestic head cloudward. There is no more impressive structure in the entire world of my experience than the tower or keep of Pembroke Castle. For one whole day I hovered about it; walked round it, studying its ivied walls; stood inside it, gazing up the giddy height from its grassy floor to its domical vault atop; climbed and clambered over and about its rugged stones, sometimes with bated breath, ever under the spell of a fascination as positive as it was novel. I found the tower was not often climbed. "Can I climb these stairs?" I asked of an attendant, pointing to the entrance of the mural stairway which wound upward in the thickness of the wall. "It is possible, sir," she replied, "but many of the steps be gone." I found it was like climbing a particularly steep hill, except that no hill would compel one to so twist and turn and grope. Part of the time I was on all fours. The central column around which these well-stairways usually wind had here quite fallen away, leaving a sinister-looking abyss, down which I looked as I clambered upward; and the stairs were but a series of projections from the stones of the tower, of which they seemed a solid part. It undoubtedly was dangerous to climb them; I should have backed out of the enterprise had not the young woman assured me it was possible to go up.

By-and-by I find a fragmentary rope dangling down the well of the absent column; it is fast at the other end to an iron ring of the battlement; with its aid I reach the top at last. It is rather exciting to stand on this height, at top of a crumbling tower (it crumbles as the ages lapse; it does not crumble visibly, any more than an oak visibly grows), with no parapet or railing of any sort, and the wind blowing such great guns from the sea that I fear they will blow me off—a thought which prompts me to sit down. I gaze awhile at the sky, the hills, the waters, the ships, and then look down into the vast green court below, where sheep and fowls are feeding, and people walking about. What an unpleasant distance to fall! I rise and walk about. The sense of peril clings to me in spite of philosophy; the tower seems to rock in the strong wind from the sea. Of course the idea is absurd, but it is impossible to dispel the fancy. Coming upon an opening in the dome—a window once, clearly—I inquisitively put my head through, first laying aside my hat, and securing it with a stone lest it should blow away. Lying at full length on my breast in the window, my head within the dome, I look down the dizzy gulf. The effect is simply terrific. Numerous floors once hung in this huge well; all are gone, and the gaze is unbroken clear to the ground. Such an effect is peculiar to dismantled structures; there is nothing of it in natural cliffs or chasms; a *human* influence is here, subtle, unexplainable, awe-compelling. To calm myself with practical details, I fall to measuring the thickness of the wall. Seven solid feet, by all that is absurd! The tower will not fall to-day. I am quite sure I feel it rock in the wind all the same. Mounting higher, I stand on top of the dome, which is a grass-plot, a mound of green. I observe no new sense of danger from this added altitude —unless it be when presently I almost walk through the window, in mistake for the stairway opening; and as I have pointed out that there are no floors inside the tower—!

Directly south of Pembroke, on the coast, is St. Gowan's Head, a promontory conspicuous in a scene of rugged grandeur. Nature here vies with story to interest mankind. History has set its stamp upon the scene since history's earliest days. Superstition has covered it with such a variety of mystic legends that they are quite unrecountable. The name St. Gowan is associated in the popular mind with Sir Gawain, the nephew of King Arthur, and in the deep hollow below the Head, where the tall cliffs tower over St. Gowan's Chapel, is a vertical cleft in the rock where Sir Gawain was hidden from his enemies by enchantment. The rock opened to let him in, closed upon him, and, when his foes were gone, opened again, remaining open forever thereafter, just as you now see it, with the impression of the saint's body still visible; for in time Gawain became a saint, and the story a miracle, through the well-known assimilative process adopted by the early Christian priests respecting pagan legends. You come down to the chapel by a flight of rude limestone steps, which, as you are incredibly informed, can not be correctly counted by mere mortal. You are shown the magic stones which ring like a bell when struck, and the reason why they ring is explained in three several legends, all equally marvellous, and quite unlike each other, about the ancient bell of the chapel. Concerning the cleft in which the saint was hidden, you are given to understand that it grows larger for a tall man and smaller for a short one; in fact, expands and contracts to fit the human figure. It is a little rusty in its joints now, seemingly, no doubt from old age, for you can with difficulty squeeze into it. But you are also told that if you make a wish while in the cleft before you turn about, your wish will be gratified; and so you wish you may grow rich, or learned, or old, or sensible, according to your most conscious lacks, and there is nothing to prove you may not have your wish before you die.

Lower down the ravine is Sir Gawain's magic fountain, which with the priests became St. Gowan's sacred well, renowned for wondrous cures of chronic ills. It is, however, now no more garnished with those votive offerings of crutches, canes, and bits of raiment which formerly made it eloquent of other people's troubles.

Now the coast becomes all broken up with curious fissures, pools, funnels, insulated rocks, arches, pillars, caldrons—a riot of eccentricity, suggesting the gambols of some old

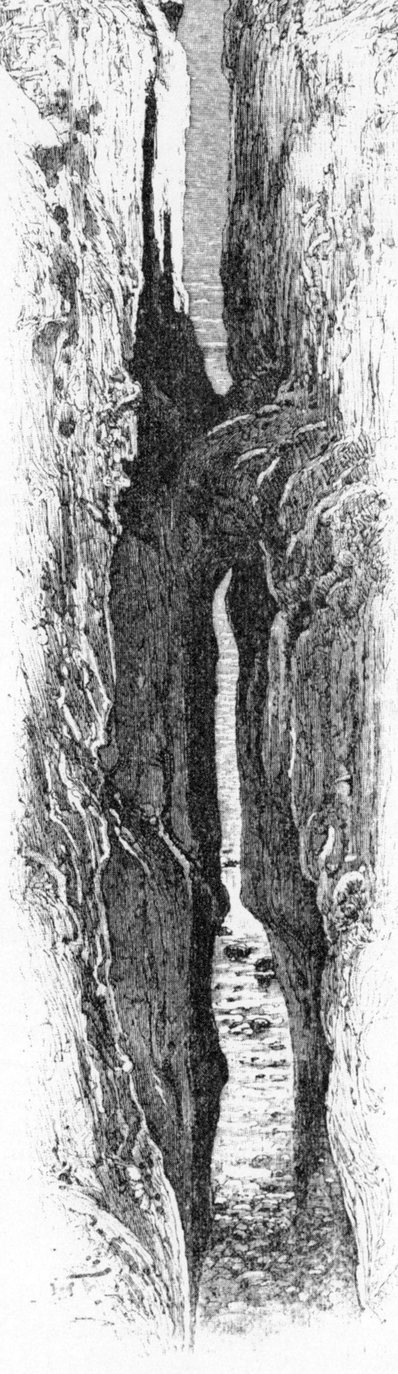

THE HUNTSMAN'S LEAP.

god of primeval mythology. To skip this part of the coast would be to do a thing which in a strong walker could have no other excuse than laziness. But you must be a strong walker indeed if you go on, for you will get no lifts over hard places; and what is more, you must carry with you whatever you mean to eat, for you will find no inns. The cliffs are the loftiest of any you have yet encountered; as you go westward they climb higher and higher. The Huntsman's Leap is one of the most striking of the cliff fissures; it gets its name from a tradition that a huntsman coming upon it in full career, did not perceive it until too late to rein in his horse. and so was compelled to jump it. Standing near the brink of this chasm, you may estimate the chances for success in such an undertaking: the gorge is sixteen or eighteen feet broad in its narrowest part, and the turf slopes abruptly to the edge; but the tradition says the huntsman got across. The sides of the chasm are perpendicular, and through the far-distant cleft at the bottom the sea is seen, with a strange light on its breast.

Beyond this chasm is a round hole in the greensward atop of the cliff, called Bosheston Meer, which leads by a slender rock-hewn tunnel or pipe down through the cliff to the sea below, about a furlong from the opening on the cliff-top. A hollow sepulchral booming eternally resounds from this weird hole, and when there is a storm the noise becomes prodigious. A column of sea-water then rushes up the pipe, and leaps through the hole high into the air with a reverberation like the firing of cannon. As the spray falls back into the hole, a vacuum is created in the air of the immediate vicinity, through which sheep are sometimes sucked into the gulf. This particular hole has considerable celebrity in Wales, but it is one of a large number of like circular cavities which are found along our route.

Milford-Haven is the remotest United States consular port in Wales, an agency subject to the Cardiff consulate. The business done here is insignificant, but the prospects of Milford-Haven are, and have long been, magnificent. Here is a harbor of really grand proportions—a land-locked harbor where all the navies of the world might ride at anchor—but time has passed it by. In earlier centuries Milford-Haven was a famous sea-port. Henry VII. landed here with his French allies when he marched through Wales to the English throne. Cromwell made this his chief war station for communication with Ireland and France. Shakspeare put Milford-Haven in his immortal story more than once. Perhaps there is no place in Great Britain which has known such remarkable vicissitudes of prosperity and adversity during the past century. Its career is typified by the *Great Eastern* steam-ship, that leviathan of the deep which was going to revolutionize travel between Europe and the United States. Here it lies now, in the shelter of Milford's graving-dock, mighty but forgotten. Yet busy and hopeful brains are still at work for Milford, planning great results in the near future. Milford is, as a matter of fact, twenty-four hours by steam-ship nearer New York than Liverpool is, and the natural advantages of her harbor are simply peerless. Can one wonder that there are sanguine souls who believe an era of prosperity is to be inaugurated here far surpassing anything in the past?

We strike across country from Milford, to resume the shore line higher up on St. Bride's Bay, and pass through Haverford-West (a town of considerable importance in this part of Wales), and under the broken walls of Roche Castle. This striking ruin marks the northwestern limit of "Little England beyond Wales." It stands on the Welsh-English border line. The Normans had no possessions, and consequently no need of castles, beyond this point. You climb to the broken ruin up a steep path; it occupies the summit of a towering mass of trap-rock which rises abruptly from the level plain. There is no like rock anywhere in sight as your eye traverses the country for miles about. A tradition of a kind met with in the folk-lore of many lands attaches to Roche Castle: that its feudal lord built it in this peculiar place because he was warned in a vision that he should die by the sting of an adder, by which fate he did die, the adder coming to him in his stronghold to seek his life.

Nothing could be more desolate than the picture presented on the breeze-blown sands of St. Bride's Bay when a storm is rising. The wild winds whistle along its cloud-hung coast, and lash the waters into a seeming fury; white-caps cover the waves which plunge landward, and drag the rattling pebbles on the shore with a noise like the snarl of eating lions; yet ships ride safely at anchor, knowing that this semblance of fury is not of a sort to frighten mariners. In most weathers the waters of St. Bride's lie in an intense calm from morning till night, and under the watching stars.

We skirt the irregular shores of the bay until we reach the limit of its northern boundary, and stand on the westernmost point of Wales—the nearest reach of original British soil toward the land of the American. This point is called Ramsey Isle, and is divided from the mainland by a strait about a quarter of a mile wide, through which the tide runs with great force, at times forming a cascade over a reef of rocks on the western side, and filling the narrower portion of the strait with whirlpools. From the strait Ramsey Isle rises. At one portion of its western face it forms a sheer cliff some four hundred feet high. Here several detached rocks or islets stand out to sea, sheltering the base of the cliff. Under their lee the sea does not break much, but lifts and

STACK ROCKS, NEAR PEMBROKE.

falls heavily, alternately roaring and snoring in the caves and crevices. With a heavy sea outside, the noise is deafening. The surface of the water is covered with a delicate lace-like reticulation of sticky foam. Thousands of gulls, razor-bills, and puffins — the birds called locally "eligoogs"—wheel round the rocks, or range themselves in interminable ranks on the ledges.

And now we are in the heart of Dewisland, most Celtic of Celtic regions, scene of the life-labors of St. David, who is to the Welsh what St. George is to the English, St. Andrew to the Scotch, and St. Patrick to the Irish. The lover of coast scenery is in his element at St. David's. The walks along the cliffs are enchanting. One can spend weeks in exploring the wild beauties of the shore, its coves and caves, its thymy promontories, the infinitely various hues and configurations of the cliffs, the smooth sands lying yellow in the sun, the seaward-gazing gorges, the pure clear water at the feet of the crags. The abundance of primeval or prehistoric antiquities scattered over this parish is so prodigious that it is simply impossible to speak of them. The mediæval remains are even more extensive. The ruined palace of the ancient bishops, which is one of the most beautiful ruins in

ST. DAVID'S.

Wales, is especially celebrated for its elegant open Gothic parapet. The palace is roofless and neglected, but extensive restorations have been made upon the cathedral, where public worship is now held as in past ages. The most impressive feature of this once mighty and influential cathedral town, to my mind, is its ruined palace, illustrating time's changes even more forcibly than the dwindled population; for this palace was one of the most splendid in Britain, and it was one of seven in this see, all nearly as grand, and all now in ruins, open to the winds of heaven and the sheep and cattle of man.

Time was when St. David's stood supreme among the cathedrals of this land. It was the shrine to which kings and conquerors made pilgrimages throughout the earlier centuries of the Christian era. After St. David's canonization, two visits to his tomb were considered equal to one to Rome, and three equalled a visit to the Holy Sepulchre at Jerusalem. The names of its great men figure splendidly in the pages of history, sacred and profane, as well as in superstitious legend and tradition. The cathedral, like that at Llandaff, lies in a deep hollow below the town, in contrast to whose insignificance and poverty the splendor of these mediæval remains bursts upon the eyes of the delighted traveller like a dream of enchantment; and the feeling is only enhanced by the desolation of the surrounding country, and the wild gloom of the rugged coast, upon whose black walls the Atlantic breaks in sullen majesty.

The land between St. David's and Fishguard is a wind-swept, treeless moor, much of it sedulously cultivated, however, the fields being sheltered by earthen banks six to ten feet high. The coast is edged with cliffs averaging perhaps one hundred feet, with here and there various rock-bound pools, in which the turmoil is wonderfully grand when a very heavy sea is running. From one of these pools, called Pwll Strodyr, a headland of great renown may be seen in the distance. Upon it the French made a landing in February, 1797, few in number, weakened by a voyage conducted under the most unfavorable circumstances (some say also by hard drinking), and surrendered to a few red-coats, believing them supported by a larger force, an astute Cymro having promenaded in the distance a number of Welsh women in their tall hats and red cloaks. The Welsh forces were under the command of Lord Cawdor, whose descendant, the present Earl of Cawdor, is Lord-Lieutenant of Carmarthenshire, the existing representative of the historic thanes of Cawdor.

This headland adjoins the town of Fishguard, or Fiscard—a dirty little fishing port with a fine natural harbor, deep, unobstructed, and well sheltered, in which large ships can take refuge in stress of weather. These numerous excellent harbors occurring at such frequent intervals along the Welsh coast are the providential antidote to the bane of its cruel cliffs. The town is made picturesque by being built partly on ground level with the port, and partly on high hills which look far out to sea. Hence sweep the wide waters of Cardigan Bay, lined for a great part of its southern boundary with cliffs of varying grandeur, which gradually diminish in height as we go northward toward Aberystwith, the limit of our present journeying.

Aberystwith may be called the Newport of Wales, as Tenby has been called its Long Branch. It is a town of some importance, quite aside from its watering-place character—thickly populated, bustling, and ancient of aspect as to its back streets, however modern and merry in its sea-facing features. Its life goes busily on in winter as in summer—the life of a sea-port town, with sailing ships and steamers trading with Liverpool and other ports—and its grand hotels on the shore awaken to life with the fashionable crowd of the bathing season. It is true that, as at most of the British sea-side watering-places, the "season" at Aberystwith lasts forever, so mild is the climate. I was frozen out there one July, all the same, and packed for home and a warm fire-side with great alacrity; but the Aberystwithians point with pride to Sir Charles Clarke, Bart., who immortalized himself by saying that "in certain cases a fortnight spent at Aberystwith will do more good than a month at any other watering-place." The significance of this Bunsby-ish remark no doubt lies in the application of it. Aberystwith is a most salubrious spot, where one is tempted to tarry long. There is a ruined castle, of course; it stands on the hill to the east of the town. In the vicinity is the renowned Devil's Bridge, and there are some splendid mountains to climb, such as Plynlimmon. When you walk out on the pier on the evening of a hot summer day, you find that the experience is a pleasant one. The pier is a frail-looking, graceful iron structure, painted red, set solidly into the rock bottom (which here conveniently exists, at the eastward end of a stretch of sandy beach), its iron feet shining with sea-weeds and incrusted with salt. There is a flight of iron stairs at the end, which leads down to and into the sea. On the pier are a number of small buildings of wood on light ornamental iron frames, prettily painted in blues, browns, and light yellows, with mahogany window-frames; and two band-houses, open on all sides to the summer night, but provided with canvas-covered walls (in pleasant weather buttoned up into the ceiling), by which they can be snugly inclosed in time of storm. The scene under the stars is lovely: the lights in the line of windows facing the sea along the crescent-shaped beach; the dark background of night-hung mountains behind the town; the rising moon throwing a gleam of silver over the rugged castle outlined strong against the eastern sky; the soft waves down below lapping musically the pier's supports, creeping softly among the huge black piles of shaggy sea-weed, gently washing the long stretch of bare rocks, sand, and shingly beach. Who could imagine this quiet babbling spirit of somnolence to be the same sea which, lashed by the storm, comes leaping up the cliffs like a pack of hounds, upjetting in spirts of wild sea-smoke and hissing fleeces of froth ?